It was the middle of the night.
Kevin and Wellington were
asleep in the kennel.

A bright light lit up the sky. Then there was a crash and a bang. Kevin woke up with a jump.

He saw another bright light. It was lightening. CRASH ... BANG. It was thunder. Kevin was frightened.

There was another bright light.
There was another CRASH ...
another BANG. Wellington woke up.

Then the rain came. It splashed into the kennel. It got deeper and deeper. Kevin and Wellington were frightened.

"Let's get out of here," said Wellington. "We must go somewhere high, away from the water."

So Wellington and Kevin went out into the wet night. Another bright light came. Another crack of thunder came.

Wellington took Kevin up the hill to the little shed. They banged on the door in the middle of the night.

Jelly and Bean let them in.

"Please may we stay here for the night?" said Wellington. "We were frightened in the kennel."

Kevin and Wellington stayed with Jelly and Bean all night. When it came light, they went back to the kennel ... but it was not there!

"igh"

night

bright

light

lightening

frightened

high

High Frequency Words

it was the of and in a up
he get we go away went to
on for said all they

were there jump with saw
another came got out here must
from water so took door them
night when then back but not
little